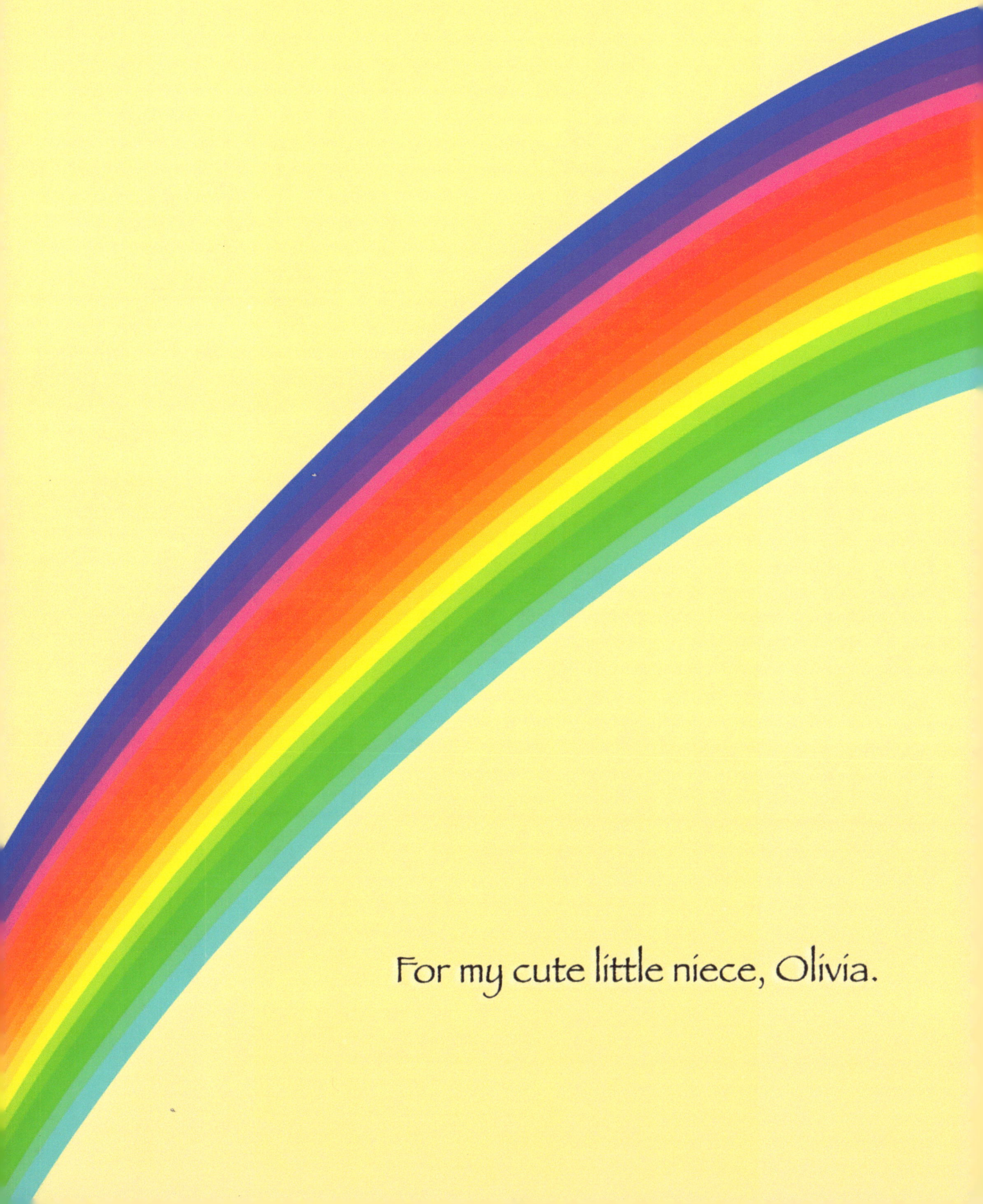

For my cute little niece, Olivia.

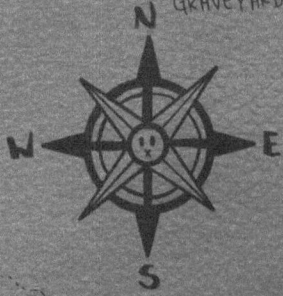

Deep in the woods lived a rabbit named Tom,
Who was taught and raised by a caring Mom.
If ever he came down with a cold or the flu,
She would make him some hot vegetable stew.

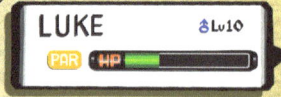

Tom had a friend named Luke the Bunny,
Who was widely known to be quite funny.
While Luke was not as brave as Tom,
His friends were there to keep him calm.

Third in the group was Fredrick the Hare,
Who challenged his friends with an amusing dare:
"Walk through the forest, to the mean Fox's lair…"
"then stand before him and give a great big stare!"
Luke warned them, "This plan is risky and outrageous!"
But Tom urged Luke to be more courageous!

So off they hopped to complete the dare,
When along the road they spied a wooden chair.
Next to it, a toy and half-eaten pear.
What in common do these objects share?
Being curious, the friends searched for more clues,
Only to be surprised by a big, scary Kangaroo!

Luke was startled and jumped fifty feet in the air!
Fredrick closed his eyes and said a little prayer.
The Kangaroo stomped on the floor with his mighty feet,
But Tom stood there brave, with a steady heartbeat.
As the huge, angry Kangaroo stamped and roared,
Tom reached for his mighty carrot sword!

One quick swipe was all it took,
To scare away that no-good crook.
Away on his mighty feet Kangaroo sped,
His image growing smaller and smaller as he fled.

The battle was frightening, they had to admit.
But they had gone much too far in order to quit.
And after picking some fruit from a pear tree,
It was time to continue on their long journey.
Three hours and three pears later,
They stumbled onto something much greater.

They froze with fear, as they saw a hawk.
And three tiny hearts went into shock.
Before having a chance to run away,
Hawk uttered something rather odd to say.
"Make me laugh, I'll make you a deal…"
"Make me mad and I'll make you my meal!"

Luke was surely fit to save this day,
Sharing laughter was always his way.
Fragile lives were in his paws,
So in his mind, a plan he draws.

Without warning they hear a "Toot!"
It seemed as though Luke ate too much fruit!

Expect that sound, Hawk did not,
And he got that laugh that he had sought.
"Pass, you may, the deed is done,"
"For I am having heaps of fun!"

TooT!

And pass they did, beyond the trees,
Grass so green, a calming breeze.
To the Fox's lair they go.
A great big stare for him they owe.

Long ago on their journey they set,
Tired the furry bunnies began to get.
"Far we've gone, let's take a rest."
"Near that bush," said Tom, "I do suggest."
Soft it was, they squeezed into a groove.
But to their surprise, it began to move!

A giant ostrich, now they did see,
Much too tall and awfully feathery!
Continued on his groovy neck,
Painted endless spotted fleck.
And at the end, a sturdy beak.
Ostrich unleashed a rowdy shriek!

"Who would dare disturb my precious sleep?"
"A grueling punishment you shall reap!"
"Now turn around from whence you came…"
"Or only you bunnies are to blame!"

Fredrick spoke, for an idea he had,
If the others knew, they'd think him mad.
"Honorable Ostrich we mean no harm."
"We're just cute little bunnies—see you no charm?"
"Adorable faces you must agree,"
"May we pass your land for free?"

"I admit those cheeks are cute and plumpy,"
"But I am afraid that I'm much too grumpy!"
"If I was well-rested, that alone might have worked,"
"But you've interrupted my sleep, so now I'm irked!"

Fredrick the Hare could not rest,
It was time he gave his very best.
"Such a Mighty Ostrich that you are,"
"To challenge you would leave us scars."

"Legends tell feats of what you hold:"
"Heads held low, under Earth's fold."
"Yet bunnies are burrowed for weeks on end,"
"Perhaps a title you hope to defend?"

With his eye, Ostrich gave a thoughtful look.
They awaited his answer as they shivered and shook.
"Challenge accepted—I will not lose."
"For I'm the best, make sure to spread the news!"

Ostrich wasted no time to meet his goal,
With his heavy beak he dug a hole.
"When all is done, congratulate me,"
"I can stay under longer, wait and see!"
Outsmarting the Ostrich, here was their chance,
They ran past the hole, they can now advance!

Suspense grew as the challenge was near,
They rubbed their eyes as the path was clear.
They quickly rushed down the rolling hill,
Their excitement could hardly keep them still.
They stood in awe of the towering stoop.
Together they huddled in a tight little group.

Suddenly, a voice came from the lair,
"You can't make me come out of here, I swear!"
"It's much too scary and dangerous outside."
"Kangaroo took my toy, forcing me to hide."
"Up high, Hawk is watching from the sky."
"And down below Ostrich will let none pass by."

The Fox didn't seem as mean as they thought.
In fact, he seemed more fearful and distraught.

They learned that their impressions were all wrong:
Tom said, "Kangaroo wasn't as tough all along!"
Luke noted, "All Hawk needed was a good laugh."
Fredrick added, "Ostrich was beat by his own gaffe!"
Fox listened and became overwhelmed with joy,
Knowing he would reunite with his favorite toy!

Overjoyed, Fox leaped out from his lair,
And took a full breath of fresh air.
Free at last, he thought, free at last!
His fear was only a thing of the past!
They celebrated and played together,
And basked in the warm Summer weather.
That fateful day, a fourth companion was made,
A dare produced a friendship that would never fade.

About the Author

T.M. Phan grew up in Northern California with three brothers and one sister. It was a close knit family where creativity was encouraged. He gained an interest in writing while taking English courses in high school and set out to write fun stories that reminded him of his childhood. His influences span many genres including video games, Japanese animation, science fiction, and classic fables. Currently, he continues to write short stories, while also running various businesses, and spending quality time with his family and friends.

www.ingramcontent.com/pod-product-compliance
Lightning Source LLC
Chambersburg PA
CBHW042018090426
42811CB00015B/1677